I0175647

FINISHING LINE PRESS
www.finishinglinepress.com

Prairie Smoke

Poems from the Grasslands

poems by

Clara Bush Vadala

Finishing Line Press
Georgetown, Kentucky

Prairie Smoke

Poems from the Grasslands

ISBN 978-1-63534-149-2 First Edition

ACKNOWLEDGMENTS

Thank you to the following publications for recognizing and publishing my work:

SLAB: Sound and Literary Art Book for "The Real Prairie"
Unsplendid for "Toads" (now "American Toad") and "Virulence"
The Seldom Review for "Well, Milnor, North Dakota" and "Longing"
Pacuare Nature Reserve 2015 Poetry Anthology for "Wolfbait"
AE: Archivation Exploration for "Skunk, Alive"

Thank you to all the professors and mentors at Texas Tech University's Honors College EVHM program for the opportunity to begin this project my senior year, for the help, encouragement, and excitement along the way, and for the chance to explore writing and the natural world, even as I prepared for vet school in the mean time. Thank you, Dr. Susan Tomlinson, for making the names of things come alive, and for making me a careful observer. Thank you Kurt Caswell, for the incredible workshop and immersive experiences that helped my writing develop immensely over the few short years I was a student at Texas Tech. A *huge* thank you to Dr. William Wenthe, as well, for his help when this project was much smaller and just beginning. Thank you to the Texas Tech University Special Collections Library (and Dr. Diane Warner) for the Sowell Collection Conference every year, a gathering that proved as inspiration time and time again. Lastly, thank you to all the family and friends who've read these poems over and over, who've cultured my love of the outdoors, and especially my wonderful husband, Adam, for his unending love and support of me and my work.

Publisher: Leah Maines
Editor: Christen Kincaid
Cover Art: Robert Nicol and Clara Bush Vadala
Author Photo: Robert Nicol
Cover Design: Elizabeth Maines

Printed in the USA on acid-free paper.
Order online: www.finishinglinepress.com
also available on amazon.com

Author inquiries and mail orders:
Finishing Line Press
P. O. Box 1626
Georgetown, Kentucky 40324
U. S. A.

Table of Contents

I. North Dakota

Field Work

One day
in the prairie
is not
full
with conversation,
but direction,
with language,
but observation:
this:
is the fullness of prairie:
imagine yourself
here, the space
in between.

Well, Milnor, North Dakota

The water itself is orange,
bubbled up in touchable
waves of iron, boiling
on the gas-lit stove-top.

I'm rusting from
the outside in, not
a purposeful hardening,
but a flaky, quarter-formed

skin of understanding.
In fingernails, pink, undernail
softskin blends to blood-orange
with exposure,

and this well feeds us,
old, but potable, drink,
drilled into the partial skeleton
of the scattered bones of grass.

This well colors us,
blotched and pitiful
and stubborn, with tattoos
of a patchy, failing, prairie,

stamps us, brightening
tendrils of strawberry
in blonde hair, with remembering:
most things here are manmade,

rust, human chemistry.
Iron becomes the way of life,
where clouds sweat rain
singly into marsh.

Proof—in stained porcelain,
white tile, the taste of it
in tap, as though the prairie
bleeds for us to live;

the well, the last artery
of the drying grassland. But we
live here, still, no one anemic,
and everyone a leech.

The Dark Clouds

I.ND

They are the whole Earth
when they come.

Pregnant with anxiety,
they flash slow, white vines of it.

They approach
together as synapses,

Zeus-brain impulses.
They are, at first, mute,

waiting, heavy with salty
humidity, calm and opaque.

II.

they fracture the whole Earth with
rain. they growl and

squeeze. They bleed
slews of segregated gray

streaks on the horizon, against
the west

window, on one side of the house.

III.MN

In lightning, the whole Earth
is colorless, and only skeletons

of the horizon remain, pale
bones of ash-gray aspen,

smacked still frames
of grassland: black

big bluestem, gray
alexanders, and bruised

prairie clovers, mottled,
wrong, undeveloped

photographs from the
dark room of the storm.

Skunk, Alive

It's 4 am, and you're as sleek as tar
It's really not your fault you're marked like roads—
Your asphalt backside broken by the white
That lines your sides above your shoulder blades—

Like you've nowhere else to be but on them,
You descend from midnight onto highways
When we forget the stench of paving roads,
Reminding us with sacrifice: that scent

That stretches miles before the wind makes you
Anonymous, again. Please, find a stream,
Be washed away in that instead of smashed
By bumpers. There's no glory in your guts,

They're only feeding hungry buzzards now
Don't you get it? I don't want to smell you.

Flight

What must it be like,
perpetual motion?
The stop-stare-run of prey:

A curious deer acting against
nature, idles near the roadside,
satellite ears in a panic, then resting.

My steps fade to the silence
of wild things—the almost
whisper of water

shooed from trampled plants.
He's lanky, young, unsure. Running
might only trip him up, slow him.

So we walk, parallel,
on two sides of a dirt street,
edgelands underfoot.

At each crunch, hunch-backed,
tense-muscled, our breath stops
together,

and what should have forced
flight, instead does rigidity.
For a moment we are both bathed in it.

Then I'm running
from the road—from the blood-slick
truck front, the hot iron stink

the clumsy slowing of it all,
brakes and breaking, the motionless
bones clicking evenly at each rib, ticking

like a grandfather's hands, the toll
of the horn, the shuddering,
new knowledge, too late—

At the stop sign, I wipe my speckled hand,
moving shades of red into themselves,
to have something to do.

The Real Prairie

It's easy to be selfish here,
the planet all grassland
and sky and no other place
but the corners of your eyes
where the light starts to dim,
too vast to absorb until
you squeeze it into your chest
in small doses—take the clouds
into your vena cava, black-eyed
susans to the right atrium,
let the tricuspid swing
shut with the wind, open
for the garter snake, a black
and yellow hose curled
in the ventricle, and the pulmonary
valve open like a hognose mouth,
swallowing prey, shut it to
the flow of flash flooding
wetlands filling the pulmonary
artery, the lungs, with fluid,
let it back again, through
the veins, with the sticky pollen
of invasives, into the left atrium,
fluttering like a kingbird's wings
leaving earth for weightlessness,
let the meadowlark sing echoes
into the left bottom chamber,
the mitral beat flapping in time,
the meaty ventricle pumping
out vibrato, the lub-dub
like the sound of a lek
of sharp-tailed grouse,
let it move into you like bluegrass
into prairie, until your whole
blood is filled up, thick
with the very piece of your world
you never want to share, building
the pressure to keep you alive.

Virulence

The sound of the prairie is the *chtcht*
of dragonflies, the soft cymbal tingling
of tick legs on tight skin—that's it—
the music of nails against bits
of flesh sticky with bug gum and itching—
the sound of the prairie, *chtcht*—
deer flies buzzing with secrets,
circling ears, landing slow and crawling.
Tick. Legs on tight skin, that's it,
all it takes to believe the invisible twitch
of ghost insects. Then, mosquitoes needling
into the sound of the prairie; the *chtcht*
is joined by the *zzzt ahh zzzt,*
and the whole chorus writhes, creeping
tick legs find tight skin. That's it,
in that moment, nothing exists
but virulence, and in the chilling
sound of the prairie, there's *chtcht,*
tick legs, tight skin, nothing else. That's it.

Four Towns

In four places at once,
a bunkhouse compass
tells the way home,

and the return address
on a love letter doesn't
matter because paper

is scarce anyway, and
it's written on a heart-leaf
from an alexander

that was half-crushed
in the mail to him;
There's no name

to name four towns
a few field's lengths
apart, and the envelope

steals addresses from
some five minute town
fifteen minutes from where

the house is; a new
kind of lost is a bottle-neck
sky where the horizon curves

up into blank blue, and
the bunkhouse sits north,
warped by waves of grass

in wind: cigar-top timothy,
writhing wet meadow,
and the leaves picked

for letters when there's
no one to find four places
at once but this love.

Hognose

Porch-shade slither-backs

The long hidden horizon people

Of the prairie

You live in the dirt

Like the hogs do

I haven't heard you squeal

But the dogs that dig

You up sure do

Love what you say to them

In the shade

You must be cold under there

You must plan for years

When to strike

Your smooshed face up

Out of a burrow

How cute how dainty how non-threatening

You seem

But your nose is your lure

Writhing and curling

All that time next to mammals

Is hard for you

Reptile

You have to eat the pests sometimes

Don’t you

Ever wonder what we taste like

Don’t the big things tease you

Doesn’t your jaw

Quiver unhinged at the thought

Of our warm blood

You must be embarrassed

Of your thin frame

And your pig face

You have no mirror but our disgust

After all

Maybe you even wish

You were warmblood sometimes too

Instead of the long vein

You are always tucked underfoot

Plant Press

—For Denise

Her hands are not strong
Enough to keep them,

So she presses on
Them with books

She read once, before,
And binds them

With belts she could wear
Once, too. She is sick

And they are pretty
Dried out. Preserved,

They are fractions
Of their former selves,

To some. But to us,
They are just as lovely,

They are beautiful, even.
And we will remember

Them, forever. We will
Miss seeing them

In fields, growing old
With the grasses,

And we will plan to see
Them again, sometime.

Three Things

I.

We are growing without roots,
Replanted places we can't stay,

We do not persevere like plants
Of the prairies do, every bit

Of their bloom anchored here,
Even dead and dying, and for what?

The rarity of their abundance,
The singleness of their home,

Perhaps this is their giving us
A lesson about travelling,

They are *mostly* roots, growing
Places we move from easily:

II.

We'll only see them there,
In their one habitat, frazzled

Glory, beating drought and flood
And farm and loneliness, even,

And we are growing knowing these
Plants will never leave here as we

Leave them, fragile and breaking
Underfoot, but we are trying, they are

Our vision for a new world formed
From an old one, a conservation

Felt, not seen, if we would just stay
Home, and leave them alone

III.

Again, and let them deepen
Their hold on the flatlands,

And be the rain-sponge of biomass
We know them to have been,

Let them recover their worth,
And their thirst, and their home,

And realize, when we do, hearts
Blooming with this new pride,

A network of arteries and veins
Filling us and keeping us, organs

In full flower, that we, staying home
Like we should, are mostly roots too.

Running in the Prairie

There is nothing

like the iron taste
of lung whine
and old wind,

stinging, released.
We believe
in our muscles

so we run
thinking we're
running, really

we hurt until
we are not done
just sweaty.

It is the blood
in our throats
that we know.

It is a wet cough
that warms us.
Tired, out of breath,

it is nothing
like what we
remember.

It is us older
and softer
and trying.

Chokecherry Wine

Seventeen
Berries left
In the tree

We checked
Yesterday
There were more

Before *Hey*!
You came with us
And you knew

They were gone
Who took them?
We don't mess

With Eric's
Trees but
Someone has

Broken this
Rule and
Choked

Branches clean
Into breaks
And heaps

Of Cherries
Supposed to
Be for wine

They taste
Like pucker
Neighbors

Can take them
But don't break
My trees!

I remember
Now
This is for her:
I've never

Made this wine
Bitter fruits
I hope it turns out

Sweet   Eric
Has just started
Dating again.

American Toad

You borrow asphalt's shimmer when it rains
at night, ignited, as your thirst becomes
your heartbeat, slaked with drizzle's drum,
by headlights. Jumping blind, you seem to hang
a moment, colored eager, smitten dumb.
Your siren sings you into tires. *Come,*
toads. Round your eyes the moon, one last refrain.

Remember camouflage and how you worked
yourselves to nothing, boring into brown,
the drought. You were perseverance, good.
Remember, what you did those years was worth
the digging, worth the way your bodies drowned
in dirt, and turned to husks, and looked for mud.

Home

Ya'll've all but
crucified my cohort's
slurs.
You
All
Have
hacked her healthy
contractions in half.

But when I told you
I was from Texas, too,
you just said, "You don't have an accent."

Let me tell you,
I've got distinct speak
stuck in me like mud.
I grew up authentic,
speaking something local,
I'm homegrown.
I'm a hot summer
seeping into your north.

I come from melted
together words, and football
talk, and *I'll come back now* to this:

I'm not slick,
slinging novelty,
because my place
is not in my mouth;
I am from that same language,
If I giddy up my speech
or not. If I always
slow-drawl-twang-spoke,
would you believe me then?

Drought

In Texas, there's a house on wooden stilts,
a banner spelling "HEARTBREAK" flaps across
the slats of porch, a *wrap-around.* They must
have felt so clever building homes like boats,
the newlyweds whose splintered hands held tight
to porch-rail prow at night, mosquito spray,
their pheromone of choice; below the house,
the crater used to be a lake, but, now,
the bowl is filmed in skins: old paint and dust,
the sloughing house a skeleton of home.

In North Dakota, wetlands leak toward
the sky instead of from it. Thigh-high pools
negate the watermarks across our throats
from years when rainfall let us swim among
the cattail inflorescenses. We must
have felt so peaceful, watching prairies fill
like bowls, remembering the lakes one state
away, in Minnesota, up here, now,
though, water isn't tall enough to reach
the grasses more than just to skim their roots.

Longing

—For Adam

If I could, I would take you
from your home

and leave you
in the sky. I would

watch you swim
among the stars each night

and blister in the sunrise
every morning

What are you waiting for?
There is nothing

but the air getting deeper
between us. Find me

in the dust in your closet
and breath me in deeply,

steal me into you with the south
wind or I'll be rooted here

like chokecherry forever.
I can see you, I think,

on the edge of every flat horizon
where the grass falls off and I can't

reach. I want to take you away
from there—

the space after space after space,
where you're barely visible, eternally,

except for your neon
memory, burned behind

my lids when I close my eyes.
I would rather lose my eyes

than forget what you look like.

Mosquito (peace keeper)

I am the sting of red
Lumps becoming: Red
Itch rising, I wonder
What you think about,
The slow seeping
Of neutrophils
Into the pinprick I make
Or the hole you finally open wide,
The wound I made,
Snout, stuck steep and strong
Into your vessels, deep, to feed
On you, bleed you,
Make you new again,
With new spit spilling into veins slack
With the tone of your Vagus nerve,
Strumming sweet tingles of nerve-song
Into your relaxed form.

Summer afternoons taste best
When you realize I'm there, lurking
Among the chiggers and grass
You forgot to mow
Before rain, and now it's too wet,
Best when your heart
Kicks in, epinephrine, pools in
Your extremities, veins, now, snug, pulled
Tight around my snout as I stay
There to drink just long enough
To touch the other side
Of your leaky vessels,
Just long enough
For you to feel me touching
Its smooth surface.

I never know how I always find them,
But they are always there,
The sweet streams of you

Filling me with something
To share the next time
Someone tries to slap
Me away but aims too late
The next time I drool
Into another wound
Some sense of me
I exist for a reason,
Needle-tipped and hungry
So hungry
No disease satiates
No blood tastes good
Ends thirst
Helps me
Only slows me down,
I am here for a reason:
I want to share you
And everyone and everything
With everyone and everything
I am peace, can't you see
The olive branch
I carry, blood,
The great keeper
Of all things living?

Setting

We are not worth
The sun. It is so apparent
Here, the whole horizon

Waking at once. Be still
While the Earth is made
Septicemic, sick with light.

The sun will not set,
Instead, spread, filling
All spaces, revealing

Even the in between
Of veins on clover leaves,
Until there's more space

Than substance, yet. Finally,
Golden-red rays, spilling
Like hemorrhage, will warm

Our hearts to furnaces,
Overwhelmed by the volume
Of hot blood invading us

Until we become blood,
Eventually; that same light
We loved seeing burnt into clouds

In the morning, at dusk,
And we'll be reabsorbed,
In that last setting sun.

Or we won't.

II. Minnesota

Tallgrass Aspen Parkland

This place is a cell:
dependent on minutia.

A glacial lake's remains
make up a cytoskeleton,

a membrane lacking
cell wall proteins.

Wetlands interspersed
create portals for diffusion,

like phospholipid layers,
the membrane moves (according to rain).

To the left an inch,
a dry-ground flower blooms:

these nodes protrude
at intervals like enzymes,

unevening the landscape.
Roots invade the cytoplasm

of the Earth, beneath
the fragile topsoil,

catalyzing conformation
changes: flowers.

Brush becomes
almost viral, its aspen

offspring lysing grassland,
forced out of the cell

in upland groves.
In lowlands, like pilli,

native blades can keep
invasives out, indicate

some health; their movement
is in their spread of seed on wind.

Diseased, this native spread
is slim, but under a microscope,

you'd see the chaperonin, wind,
bending pollen from its parent,

folding into a finished complex—
an empty flower's ovary made viable.

Dog (For Boo)

I.
who sits, alone, under the house,
whispering to herself
obscenities
that she would remain
calm—

in a thunderstorm, I'm afraid
she might forget to move
and just lie there instead,
happy, in her mud, while water fills her up
and soaks the foundation

maybe this has always been her plan—

is not the same

II.
who sits, alone, beneath the porch,
whispering to the snake,
stories
that she tells no one
else—

she gives chase to deer, ducks
with too much zeal
to keep her fourth leg,
torn ACL, sound enough to use,
just fine on three

maybe she has never had to plan—

is not the same

III.
who bites your ankles when you pass,
whispering, that she might catch

the fear of you,
run, run,
run—

Minnesota has too much space for dogs
they are not afraid
of anything there but being tame,
and dying without flashing
their wild teeth

maybe they will herd forever; they have no kind of plan—

is not the same

IV.
as any other dog who
sits and whispers
sneaking into silence,
crawl on all fours,
elbows, now, the mud,
beneath me, bring
your coil beneath me,
I will protect you,
come herd, and I will
not separate you,
believe me,
It's alright when I die,
I am not yours anymore.

CAUTION: DO NOT APPROACH WILDLIFE

Leave the wild alone like you would
not come between mothers
and their children

Close Encounters

There are black iron bears
At each county exit, flat
Against the aspen backdrop,
And half in the trees.

It's funny how these still
Forms feel real every time,
Dark lump cutouts, midnight
Negatives in daytime.

But real bears move,
Even if only in the glint
Of their hairs, subtle
Muscle ripples. *Crunch.*

Twigs. Big-bluestem parted
Then each meristem flicked
Straight as it passed, invisible
But for its sound. Listening,

I heard a cub cry like an old
Windmill (after having been still)
Starting its cutting into
the sky. I wanted to see one.

But before the next padded paw
Hit soil, I'd already found
The shortest sedges I could see,
And ran. The brush was too thick

To glance back for pursuit,
And the birch canopy
Darkened the scene,
But when I stopped

In the reed canary,
I still tried to study columns,
All the long dark outlines,
for any glint of shifting black iron.

Moose Country

There's a place in the north
where the moose used to go.

It's empty now, but for people:
old women who shout

"what's your blood sugar level?"
men who play pool at The Eagle,

and the smattering of youth,
too much bored with life to enjoy it.

This place burns with suspicion, steeples
loom between houses. At the park,

there's a fiberglass statue on a mini-golf
green—a moose with glass eyes,

the trophy of a lost era, a participation
ribbon from nature, pinned without

permission. The way it stares,
at more than the town, it mourns,

past all the work of machines,
a shrine losing out to the churches.

Butterflies in a Petri Dish

It's like clapping when you catch them
But they aren't squashed
It's a miracle
Really
        Catch and release
Like children
        Catch and release
We
Lure them
Just to look at them
Just to see them squirming
Orange and black, we hail them, monarchs.

Wolfbait,

they called her
sagging radio
collar
knobbed joints
lob her
forward, or back,
who knows anymore
where she
came from or what for.

Wolfbait's skin
is nicked from barbed
wire fence
lines she climbs
over, thin
frame splayed
over flat fields, car dealerships
long behind where
she's been left, working her way home.

Wolfbait only wants
one thing,
to find the dents
she made and fit back
into them, bend
back into herself
into the half-formed
moose-butt she rubbed
into that old green Subaru.

Wolfbait maybe
wants two things,
the other being
to bite the woman stupid
enough to beat
her with a purse
to keep

her rhubarb intact, to leave
them no choice but to take her,
track her,
tranquilize her, find her bones later,

because there are wolves
out there,
Wolfbait.

Still Life: Coyote and Cranes

Listen to this slow sculpture:
the seasons have stopped
spiraling, the animals
have stopped creeping

their lines in the grasses
and have taken up stalking,
still as grey, smooth as the blue
feathers of these herons

whose bodies are fast,
fashioned to last season's
cattail stalks, stilts. There
are two and they will rot

there, as long as they are
being watched. And coyote's
moonlight serenade is silence,
as long as the herons,

being watched, know he's
watching them. His lover
will leave him and yip,
lonely, at his stone

figure, in paralyzing pursuit,
in frozen sacrifice. The coyote
knows his slipping would move
the world. And he can *feel*

silence now, in the middle
of the day. Two herons,
coyote. Beyond the predator
and prey becoming fossils,

the horizon is broken by paper-
barked aspen; they sit between

two groves in a blank field.
Drawn close by surrounding

space, their fierce agreement
exposed, they are hearts
and each the other's arteries.
There is no word to make them move.

Arson

Last year, uncontrolled, a fire jumped the road
of a one-street town, toward the daycare.
Before that, the old crewhouse burned down.

These fires start when the burn crew gets bored,
when trees start to sprout up out of their ash
like skeletons waiting to regrow their flesh,

when nothing but dark brown horizon stretches
flat to last year's burn line. If all strays
were fires spawned from nature, would we

forgive impatience? Is the principle enough,
that arson isn't arson when a person's life is fire—
What is there to do when the grasslands burst

with life, anyway, but burn them down and watch
them grow up again? Nothing beautiful in survival
minus any threat. Burn crews know this, but we don't

remember what we had to tear down to build up
our homes. We get bored (inside), and cold,
and that dark weather that deceived us

with winter's bright reflections, makes us set ourselves
aflame. We're our own angry stove, stomach set
to boiling over. *Warm us up.* Who hears our demands?

Fire season crews in grasslands, flaming the hearth
of the earth, our fireplace, lit by the ones
who burn to bring things alive. So who cares

if last year's fire season began because a cigarette
blew up a crewhouse ashtray? Who could
blame the smoker for every little fire he inhales?

Brush

You can feel it tickling
into tiny whorls of scabs,

Turning slowly into bark,
your skin is hypersensitive

to the ugly regrowth
working scars, scattered

tracts of infiltration,
not supposed to be

there, but there anyway,
sketching fuzzy lines

where smooth ruled
once, pale, and freckled,

grooved like aspen:
softly, and natural,

eventually your skin
is toughened to it,

calloused, hard, brown,
knobbed like the new

bark spread, the short,
sharp, blanket—brush

covering and covering,
covering and covering.

Music

Cicadas sound like stereo static
and skippers skiff exposed skin
in down beats. There is already
a rhythm in the movement
of the prairie, and sandhill cranes
squall prehistoric between the eastern
peewee's downslur and the haunt
of loonsong. There is already music
in the plains, harmonies whose overtones
are insects. Look down: slick leap
of leopard frogs like swing-low waltz tunes,
wren twitch and grass shuffle cymbal
roll, snow-sprinkled (pollen-culled)
pantlegs, small earth cloth hearth,
seedlings sporing out of spring,
on you—this is on you—this
is nature's cadence creating summer.

Into the Road (Ruffed Grouse)

You, rough and quibbling,
If you picked a puff
Of rough prairie plumage,
Would be safe, grouse.

Instead, stupid as gizzards,
Your tail feathers freed
From side-road prairie,
You wobble, brood in tow,

Your hatched clutch following.
We thought you'd be cautious
So we stopped the Chevy,
Gave you time to get away.

Then, we tried to chase you off,
Things to do that day,
But you just lined your chicks
Up and windmilled your trunk legs,

Pushing up dust and some false
Semblance of speed, ball of bird,
We had to laugh, our truck barely
Breaking five miles an hour,

While you slit your beady eyes
And lunged your necks, reaching,
Hoping we'd notice your straining
"They're racing us. *They are racing us.*"

Red Truck

We called the cops on a mailman

There was this red truck beating up the asphalt
In the town, turns out
He was just the mailman, but I didn't see a mailbox
Every place he stopped

Behind me, looking out the window rolled down,
Elbow angled at me,
Like a wave, but noncommittal, hard to remember
Unless you're suspicious

Already. I have never been seen before now,
Running roadside, miles
Before I turned around to go back crewhouse
Ways. I'm not that fast

Compared to this red truck moseying along.
Sherriff trusts this old guy
Delivering mail, but maybe he just
trusts me less.

Trailblazer, 1998

You are the drab kind
of handsome, the desperate
kind of pleasurable.
You are gray leather
sticking to thighs even
through jeans on a hot day.
You are terrible
and worth it all
at once.

You're dirty, too,
but my coworkers like you
because you're just big
enough for what they need
to do. I guess you were
therapy, or maybe just old
enough to work
to teach them that the first law
of field work is don't do
the crew.

Wild Strawberries

Everywhere, this time of year,
Are little fruit hats missing flesh,
Missing fingertip-sized treats,
Simply stems, at first

They are plenty, thin red veins,
Plump with clots of berries,
Exposed at every half-step
Through the high ground

But the bears love them
With a fierce precision, leaving
None and you wondering:
How could they be so delicate?

With fruits the width of a claw point,
so tender, so full of scarlet syrup,
in their paws, fragile and momentary,
so sweet.

Rodeo

This show is a funeral.

Bull-riding replacing watching
the hooved herds of older days
mull through, when fenceposts
and prairies did not know one another.

This is where the moose reign(ed).

Today's soil kicked up is the same
As the earth turned over before
By even-toed ungulates tens of feet
tall, probably, now, dust themselves.

Why do we all feel such joy?

At the rodeo, Scandinavian
children make beautiful faces, eyes
brimmed with clear blue irises and spilling
into out-of-towners. They look,
rather than tan, covered in pale
arena dirt, as if they have just
finished digging. This is all they know.

Justice (Public Hunting)

If you hit a cell phone tower
with a shotgun, drunk,
and at night, to watch the sparks

fly—metallic embers in a place
struck flammable by drought—
you could probably hit a deer

by daylight, sober, down
the population—public hunt,
or you're one more shotgun

shy of revenue during season
which matters more, the felony
damage (tens of thousands),

or your spot on the front lines,
killing—because who knows
what you do with things you shoot—

for the common good? In a town
of forty-eight, they never found
you, or anyone to suspect, no

sheriff's inkling stare even
swerved your way the way
you swerved home, satisfied.

Javelina

There was talk of wolverines
At Karlstad's park office
Another lady and her small dog
Wimpering about the yard.

They aren't here. They laughed.
But I remembered something
Texas taught me, about viciousness
And being cautious: Javelinas

On a park trail, I was told,
on a Big Bend bird walk,
another lady and her small dog,
had to part, not to scare the birds.

Convenience tied the poodle
To a fencepost nearby.
She was warned: the terrible pigs
Of park site nightmares.

They aren't here. She laughed.
But she forgot her poodle there,
And binoculars around her neck,
Was cautious walking bird trails.

Javelinas: being cautious
Taught her about viciousness,
They left that leash tied round
A fencepost, and only the bones

The pigs couldn't eat, and
They were gone by the time
She walked back, whistling,
Poodle, poodle. Never believing.

Tick

Where were burn ticks to kill them:

it's ick's lit wicks

lit wicks kill it it sticks

lit wick it sticks

kill ticks it's ick lit it

Waiting

We, for years and years,
have been gathering

the language of waiting:
deaf rhythms, heard faint

in muscle drum and heart
beat, the three-four we all

swing to, the dewdrop cradled
in the incomplete, between

a grass blade's tip and soil,
our necks always bent away

from the rising sun, our bodies
almost circles, crouched so low

toward the ground, we've felt
the sleep-tingle of blood heavy

limbs breathing blood back again
in crescendos, the same way,

we hope, prairie plants will recover,
we hope they are simply asleep.

Finding a Poweshiek

Skipping,
the chance
is at most the inverse
of the distance
between fences
covered,
in one week
in July,
if looking
for white lines.

Prairie Smoke

Sticktight fruits cling to clothes
like smoke potpourri; flowering,

they are gray-pink, soft tangled feelers,
hirsute placeholders for July blooms,

wisps of rose-smelling wildness,
singularly crisp and blurred;

dead, they leave skeletons of spindly
brown on beds of fanned leaves

while wood lilies litter fields
like tiny, frozen fireworks,

blazing stars spew purple fringe,
and clovers burn with bright pollen

embers; come spring, the prairie
is smoking again with the blushing

veins of afterimage left behind
for all those months, but not forgotten.

Clara Bush Vadala grew up in Celina, Texas, and also in campsites across the state on family summer trips and camping with friends. She found her writing spark at Texas Tech University, studying to go to vet school while earning a degree in Environment and the Humanities. She credits her undergraduate major and parent's musical genes (rocker dad) and poetic tendencies (award-winning poet mom) for her love of poetry and the musicality and lyricism of nature writing. Animals have also played a major role in discovering and exploring wildness, a theme she also explores in her writing and her professional life. Clara is currently a veterinary student at Texas A&M University's College of Veterinary Medicine, studying small animal and exotic veterinary medicine. She has pets of her own too, who serve as daily inspiration and animal therapy: her two dogs, Lulu and Zeus; her cat, Treble; her cockatiel, Kenneth; and an array of tropical fish. *Prairie Smoke: Poems from the Grasslands* is Clara's first full-length book of poetry.

www.ingramcontent.com/pod-product-compliance
Lightning Source LLC
Chambersburg PA
CBHW070551090426
42735CB00013B/3150